I Like to Draw!
DINOSAURS
and
OTHER PREHISTORIC ANIMALS

by Rochelle Baltzer   Illustrated by James Penfield

Looking Glass Library
An Imprint of Magic Wagon
www.abdopublishing.com

www.abdopublishing.com

Published by Magic Wagon, a division of ABDO, PO Box 398166, Minneapolis, Minnesota 55439. Copyright © 2015 by Abdo Consulting Group, Inc. International copyrights reserved in all countries. No part of this book may be reproduced in any form without written permission from the publisher. Looking Glass Library™ is a trademark and logo of Magic Wagon.

Printed in the United States of America, North Mankato, Minnesota.
102014
012015

 THIS BOOK CONTAINS
RECYCLED MATERIALS

Cover and Interior Elements and Photos: iStockphoto, Thinkstock

Written by Rochelle Baltzer
Illustrations by James Penfield
Edited by Tamara L. Britton, Megan M. Gunderson
Cover and interior design by Candice Keimig

Library of Congress Cataloging-in-Publication Data

Baltzer, Rochelle, 1982- author.
  Dinosaurs and other prehistoric animals / written by Rochelle Baltzer ; illustrated by James Penfield.
     pages cm. -- (I like to draw!)
  Includes index.
  ISBN 978-1-62402-081-0
1. Dinosaurs in art--Juvenile literature. 2. Prehistoric animals in art--Juvenile literature. 3. Drawing--Technique--Juvenile literature. I. Penfield, James, illustrator. II. Title.
  NC780.5.B35 2015
  743.6--dc23
                         2014033915

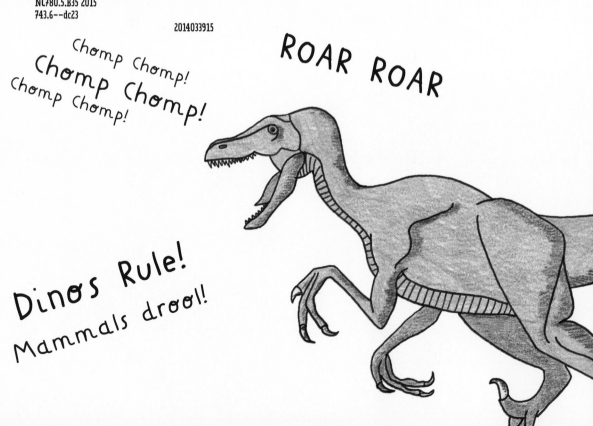

TABLE of CONTENTS

DINOSAURS and OTHER PREHISTORIC ANIMALS

For more than 150 million years, dinosaurs ruled the earth! These prehistoric **reptiles** died out about 65 million years ago. Some animals that live today resemble them. Scientists study **fossils** to find out more about these massive monsters. Let's learn how to draw some cool dinosaurs and prehistoric animals!

STUFF YOU'LL NEED

Pencil

Paper

Eraser

Marker

Colored Pencils

KNOW THE BASICS

SHAPES

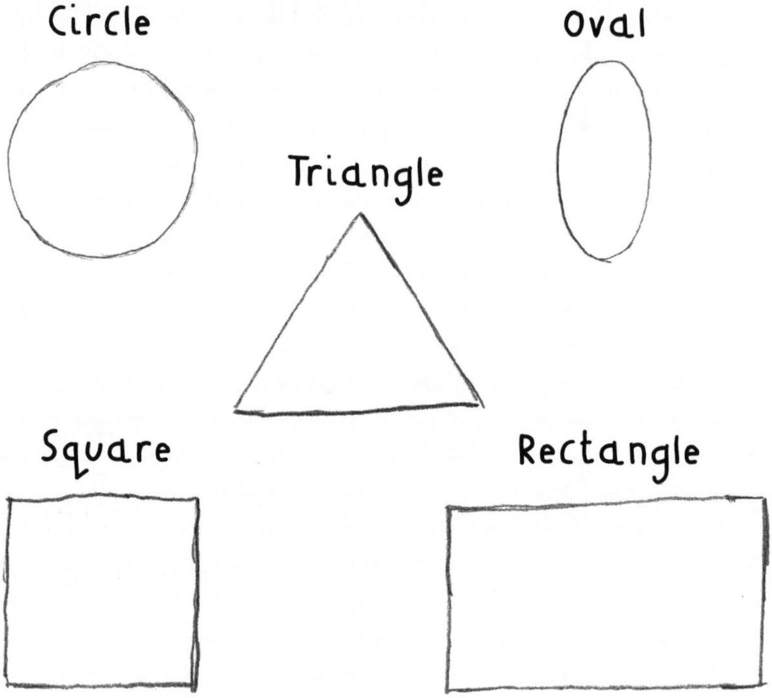

Circle

Oval

Triangle

Square

Rectangle

LINES
thick & thin

Straight

Wavy

Jagged

TALK LIKE AN ARTIST

Composition

Composition is the way parts of a drawing or picture are arranged. Balanced composition means having an even amount of parts, such as lines and shapes.

Unbalanced

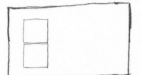

Balanced

Dimension

Dimension is the amount of space an object takes up. Drawings are created on a flat surface and have length and width but not depth. So, they are two-dimensional. You can give an object depth by layering colors and adding shadow. This makes it look like it's popping off the page!

Without Dimension

With Dimension

Shadow

Shadow is created by the way light shines on an object. Look outside on a sunny day. See how the sunlight shines on a tree? The side of the tree with more sunlight appears lighter than the other side.

Without Shadow

With Shadow

TYRANNOSAURUS REX
(tuh-ra-nuh-SAWR-uhs REHKS)

The mighty T. rex was one of the largest meat-eating dinosaurs. It weighed up to 8 tons (7.3 t) and could reach 42 feet (13 m) long! The T. rex walked on strong back legs and had short front legs. It chomped on prey with its powerful jaw. Scientists believe it could scarf down 500 pounds (227 kg) of meat in one bone-crushing bite!

1 Draw a circle for the head, an oval for the body, and shapes for the jaws.

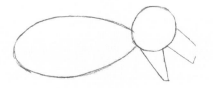

2 Draw lines for the legs and arms. Add the long tail.

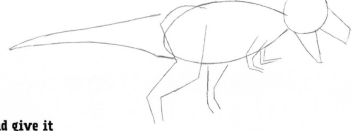

3 Add details to the head and give it teeth. Finish outlining the arms and legs, but don't detail them yet.

4 Now, add claws to the arms and legs. Finish detailing the face and body.

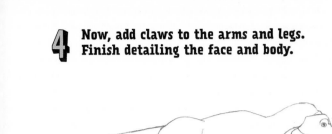

ART TIP
Make your T. rex's teeth big or small, depending on how ferocious you want it to be!

5 Outline the finished drawing with a thin, black marker.

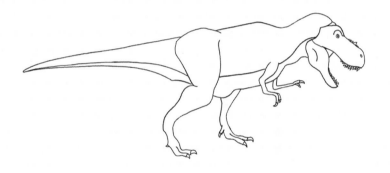

6 Color your T. rex in green and yellow tones, dark or light!

Ruler of Them All
Tyrannosaurus rex means "king of the **tyrant** lizards" in Latin.

VELOCIRAPTOR
(vuh-LAH-suh-rap-tuhr)

The Velociraptor was a small, but smart dinosaur. It was about 6 feet (2 m) long and 3 feet (1 m) tall. Scientists believe it was so intelligent because its brain was large compared to its body size. The Velociraptor ran fast on its back legs, reaching speeds of up to 24 miles per hour (39 km/h)! Each back foot had a curved claw used to slash prey.

1 Draw a circle for the head, lines for the neck, and an oval for the body. Add shapes for the jaws.

2 Since this Velociraptor is on the move, draw legs and arms in a running motion. Imagine how it would look running through the forest. Also draw in a tail.

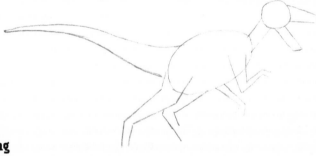

3 Add detail to the head, including teeth. Outline the arms and legs.

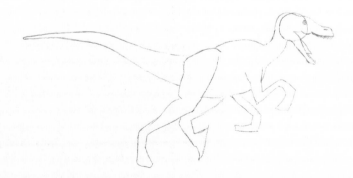

4 Finish adding details to the head. Detail the arms and legs, including claws. Finally, add details to the body to give this dino some dimension.

ART TIP
By changing the placement of the dino's arms and legs, it will look like it's running very fast or walking very slowly!

5 Outline the finished drawing with a thin, black marker.

6 Give this Velociraptor dark green skin to protect it when it's running through the forest!

Feathery Dino
Recent study suggests the Velociraptor had feathers.

STEGOSAURUS
(ste-guh-SAWR-uhs)

The Stegosaurus was a large, plant-eating dinosaur. It could grow to 30 feet (9 m) long and weigh about 2 tons (1.8 t). The Stegosaurus is known for the triangle-shaped bony plates that ran down its back. At the front of its mouth was a beak. To defend itself, the Stegosaurus likely swung its tail, which had two pairs of sharp spikes at its tip.

1 Draw a large oval for the body, a small circle for the head, and a small shape for the snout.

2 Draw triangles for the plates on the Stegosaurus's back and tail. Add lines for the legs.

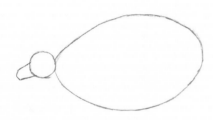

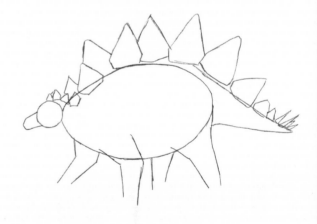

3 Outline the legs, erase the oval for the body, and add detail to the head.

4 Add final details to the legs and feet. Make sure you draw rolls of skin around the neck, and finish the head.

ART TIP

Change the shade of color on the plates to make them look like they're pointing in different directions. Add lighter tan for highlights and darker tan for shadows.

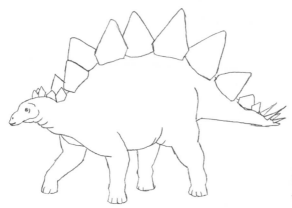

5 Outline the finished drawing with a thin, black marker.

6 Pick your own shade of green and color in your Stegosaurus! Add lighter tan to color its plates to finish it off!

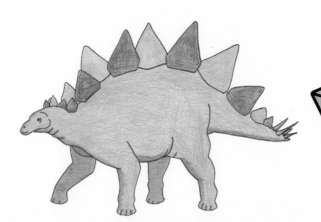

Plates with Purpose

Scientists think the Stegosaurus's plates helped the dinosaur stay at the right temperature, scare away predators, or attract mates.

TRICERATOPS
(treye-SEHR-uh-tahps)

The Triceratops was a huge horned dinosaur. Its body could reach about 30 feet (9 m) in length and could weigh up to 5 tons (4.5 t). It had two horns above its eyes and one on its nose. At the back of its head was a **frill** of bone that was 6 feet (2 m) wide! The front of its mouth formed a beak, which it used to pull and tear apart plants.

1 Draw a medium-sized circle for the head and a medium-sized oval for the body. Add lines for the snout.

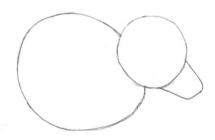

2 Add lines for the legs and tail, so the dino looks like it's walking.

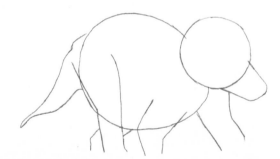

3 Detail the head by drawing three horns, an eye, a mouth, and a bony plate above its face. Also outline the legs and feet.

4 Detail the legs, feet, and face. Don't forget to add lines to the body to give it dimension.

ART TIP
Take a look at the eye on this Triceratops. The tiny white dot on the eye makes it look real and adds character to this three-horned dino!

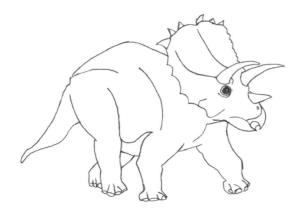

5 Outline the finished drawing with a thin, black marker.

6 Pick a shade of green to color this Triceratops! Since its horns are made of bone, they can remain white. Give them dimension by shading part of them with a dark color.

A Sight to Scare
The Triceratops used its horns and frill to defend itself against predators, such as the T. rex.

BRACHIOSAURUS
(bra-kee-oh-SAWR-uhs)

The Brachiosaurus was a gigantic plant-eating dinosaur with a long, giraffe-like neck. The Brachiosaurus could be more than 75 feet (23 m) long and weigh up to 80 tons (73 t)! Its long front legs and 30-foot (9-m) neck allowed it to nibble on the leaves of treetops. These features also made it able to see predators from far away.

1 Draw an oval for the body and a small circle for the head. Spread them apart enough to add lines for the long neck. Also add a shape for the small snout.

2 Add the long tail and lines for the legs.

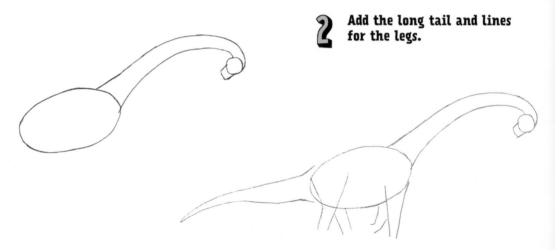

3 Outline the legs and add detail to the head, including flat teeth.

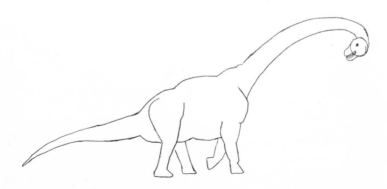

4 Add final details to the head and legs. Give the body dimension by adding long running lines that follow the underside of the neck, body, and tail.

ART TIP
The harder you push on your pencil, the thicker and darker your line will be.

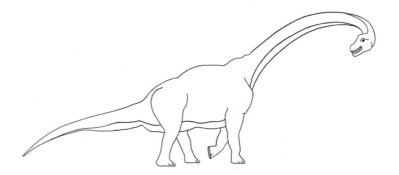

5 Outline the finished drawing with a thin, black marker.

6 Color this dino with shades of green. Don't forget a nice shade of red for its tongue!

Leggy Lizard
Long front legs earned this dino its name. *Brachiosaurus* means "arm lizard" in Latin.

ANKYLOSAURUS
(ang-kuh-loh-SAWR-uhs)

The Ankylosaurus was a broad, slow-moving dinosaur covered in armor. Its armor was made of bony plates on its head, back, and tail. At the end of its tail was a thick clump of bone, which the Ankylosaurus swung to defend itself. The Ankylosaurus could be 33 feet (10 m) long and weigh 4 tons (3.6 t). It used its small beak and teeth to eat plants.

1 Draw a long oval for the body and a small circle for the head. Add a small shape for the snout.

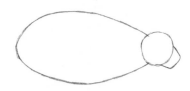

2 Give this dino short legs. Add its tail with a club at the end.

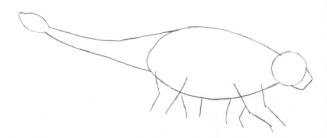

3 Add short spikes to the shell over the dino's body. Detail the head and outline the legs.

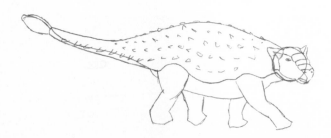

4 Finalize the spikes on the shell and the club on the end of the tail. Finish detailing the legs and the head.

ART TIP

Have fun drawing the short spikes on the Ankylosaurus's shell by drawing them all a little differently. This will make the final drawing look more like how the dino looked in real life!

5 Outline the finished drawing with a thin, black marker.

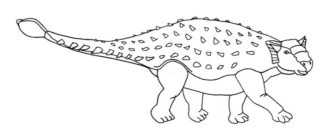

6 This dino's shell and body are two different colors! A medium brown and green work great. Leave the short spikes white and give them shadow by adding a dark color to one edge of each spike.

Heavy-Duty Armor

The Ankylosaurus's armor protected it against the powerful T. rex. Predators would have had to flip over the dinosaur to injure it.

19

PTERANODON
(tuh-RA-nuh-dahn)

The Pteranodon was a flying **reptile**. Its **wingspan** was 23 feet (7 m)! The Pteranodon ate fish with its long, pointed beak. The **crest** at the back of its head may have helped it balance or steer while flying. Pteranodon **fossils** have been found near water, and scientists believe their lifestyle was similar to a pelican's.

1 Draw a circle for the head, an oval for the body, and lines that connect the two for the neck. Add two narrow triangles for the crest and the beak.

2 This dino has arms and legs, but its arms are part of its wings. Draw short legs off the bottom of the body and long arms out to the sides.

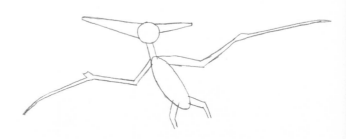

3 Add details to the head and outline the wings and legs.

4 Give this Pteranodon a mouth and nostril. Finish the wings and legs so it's ready to take off!

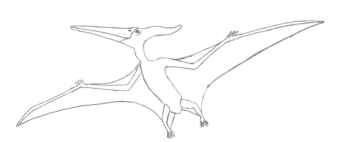

ART TIP
Draw the Pteranodon with its wings spread wide, so you can imagine it flying high above the other dinos!

5 Outline the finished drawing with a thin, black marker.

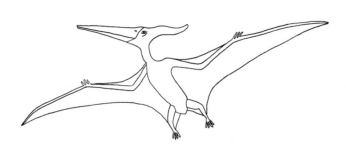

6 This Pteranodon comes in shades of blue and purple! Pick one color for a highlight and one for a lowlight. This dino is ready to launch!

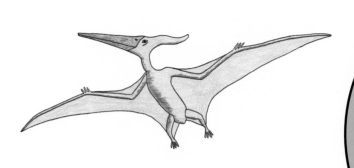

Hang Gliders
The Pteranodon was large, so it most likely soared instead of flapping its wings.

ICHTHYOSAURUS
(ihk-thee-uh-SAWR-uhs)

The Ichthyosaurus was a fishlike **reptile**. Like a dolphin, it lived in water but breathed air. It was about 10 feet (3 m) long. Its pointed snout, flippers, fin, and tail allowed it to swim fast! The Ichthyosaurus used its large eyes to find fish and other sea animals to eat.

1 Draw a circle for the head, an oval for the body, and a triangle for the snout.

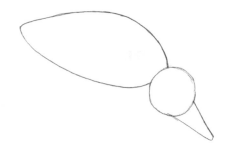

2 The Ichthyosaurus was a swimmer, so add flippers, a fin, and a tail to its body.

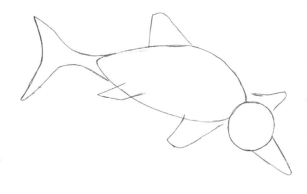

3 Outline the flippers and add details to the head and body, including an eye and the start of the mouth.

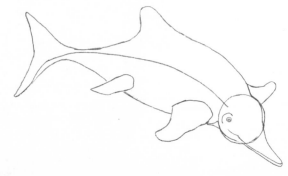

4 Finish the flippers, fin, tail, and body. Add curved lines on the head to represent folds in the skin.

ART TIP
This creature lived in the water, so the only shadow would be on the bottom of its body, because the sun was always above it!

5 Outline the finished drawing with a thin, black marker.

6 An underwater creature, this swimmer is blue. Use a darker blue for shading!

Eye See You
One type of ichthyosaur had eyes that were up to 10 inches (25 cm) across!

WOOLLY MAMMOTH

The woolly mammoth was a massive **mammal**. It could weigh up to 9 tons (8.2 t) and stand as tall as 14 feet (4 m)! The woolly mammoth had long hair on its body to keep it warm in the **Ice Age**. Like an elephant, it had a trunk and two **tusks**. It used its long, sharp tusks to dig deep in snow. Woolly mammoths ate grass and other plants.

1 Draw a circle for the head, an oval for the body, and a curved trunk.

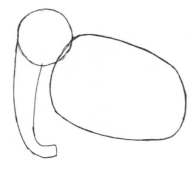

2 Add the mammoth's powerful tusks and draw lines for its strong, stable legs.

3 Detail the mammoth's coat, its head, and the end of its trunk. Also outline the legs.

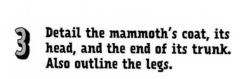

4 Finalize details on the trunk and legs. Finish the head, including the ear.

ART TIP

You can draw in the mammoth's fur easily by using a jagged or wavy line as your outline. This will give the illusion of a thick, textured coat.

5 Outline the finished drawing with a thin, black marker.

6 Give this woolly mammoth its famous woolly fur by coloring it brown! Shadow its massive tusks by coloring the bottom edges with a dark color.

Mammoth Meat

Woolly mammoths lived at the same time as prehistoric people. People hunted them for food.

SABER-TOOTHED CAT

The saber-toothed cat was a powerful predator and distant relative of modern cats. It was named for the two sharp teeth extending from its upper jaw. This **mammal** could open its mouth wide and tear through prey with its 8-inch (20-cm) teeth. It most likely hunted large, slow-moving animals such as mammoths.

1 Draw an oval for the body, a circle for the head, and lines to connect the two for the neck. Add shapes for the jaws.

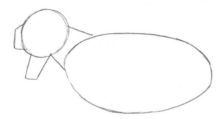

2 Draw lines for the legs and a small outline of the cat's tail.

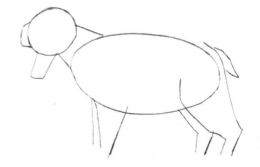

3 Add detail to the head, including ears, an eye, a nose, and those famous saber teeth! Also finish outlining the legs and feet.

4 Detail the head and legs so this cat is ready to roll. Don't forget the whiskers!

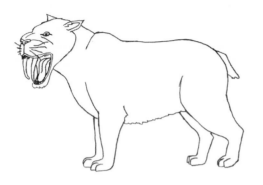

ART TIP
You can make the cat look more or less ferocious based on how many teeth you show!

5 Outline the finished drawing with a thin, black marker.

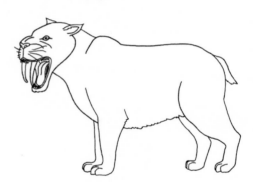

6 The saber-toothed cat's fur was a light color, close to tan, brown, and yellow. Pick out a lighter color for the highlighted parts and a darker color for the shadows. Don't forget the red tongue behind its teeth!

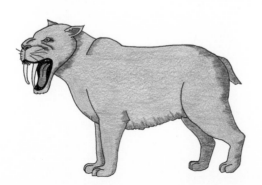

Cunning Cats
Saber-toothed cats did not chase their prey. Instead, they crept up on it, hid, and then pounced.

LOOK WHAT YOU CAN DRAW!

The Dirt on DINOSAURS

Scientists do not know for sure why dinosaurs died out. Some believe it is related to temperature, an asteroid, or volcanic eruptions.

Scientists study fossils to learn about prehistoric animals. The fossils include bones, eggs, teeth, and even poop!

Today's snakes, crocodiles, lizards, and birds are distant relatives of dinosaurs.

Dinosaur fossils have been found on every continent of the world.

Some dinosaurs may have lived up to 100 years!

The earliest birds existed about 150 million years ago. They had feathers and wings, but they also had teeth and claws!

Glossary

crest – a growth of flesh or feathers on the head of an animal.

fossil – the remains of a very old plant or animal commonly found in the ground.

frill – the hard plate on the back of a Triceratops's head.

Ice Age – a period of time between 1.8 million years ago and 11,500 years ago that includes several ice ages. An ice age is a time when thick ice sheets cover large areas of land.

mammal – a member of a group of living beings. Mammals make milk to feed their babies and usually have hair or fur on their skin.

reptile – a member of a group of living beings. Reptiles have scaly skin and are cold-blooded.

tusk – a long, large tooth that sticks out of an animal's mouth.

tyrant – a cruel ruler.

wingspan – the distance from one wing tip to the other when the wings are spread.

Websites

To learn more about I Like to Draw!, visit **booklinks.abdopublishing.com**. These links are routinely monitored and updated to provide the most current information available.

Index

DATE DUE

			PRINTED IN U.S.A.